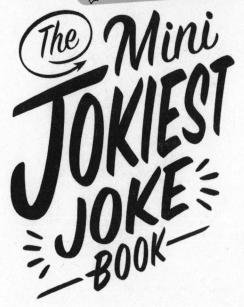

The Mini Jokiest Joke Book

JOKES BY **KATHI WAGNER**
ILLUSTRATIONS BY **AMANDA BRACK**

CASTLE POINT
BOOKS

www.castlepointbooks.com

The Castle Point Books trademark is owned by Castle Point
Publishing, LLC. Castle Point books are published and distributed
by St. Martin's Press.

978-1-250-27033-7 (trade paperback)
978-1-250-27034-4 (ebook)

Our books may be purchased in bulk for promotional, educational,
or business use. Please contact your local bookseller or the
Macmillan Corporate and Premium Sales Department at
1-800-221-7945, extension 5442, or by email at
MacmillanSpecialMarkets@macmillan.com.

First Edition: May 2020

10   9   8   7   6   5   4   3   2   1

To my Dad, who tells the best jokes,

and my Mom, who always listens

CONTENTS

What did one sheep say to the other
after being apart a long time?

Why haven't I heard from ewe?

Why did one video game get so mad at the other one?
It was trying to controller.

Why was the deck of cards so sad?
Someone stole their hearts.

Why did the fence like the sheep?
Because it was around them a lot.

How did the playing card dress up?

It wore a suit!

What did the two controllers say when the console's light turned green?
Game on!

How do you know when a goat isn't sure if you are serious?
It asks if you're kidding.

Why did the track shoes up and leave?
They were tired of running around in circles.

What do you get when you put two baby goats together?
Just a couple of kids.

What do you call an upside-down video game?
Game OVER.

Why do cats like to play video games?

Because they have nine lives!

What did the stream name its baby?
Brook.

How do you know when an Xbox has really changed?
It does a 180 instead of a 360.

Why were a tic and a toe losing the fight?
They were missing attack.

Why did the game player have to change his underwear?
They were too titan him.

What do controllers say when the game is over?
Thumbs up!

Why did the tow truck come to the arcade?

One of the games crashed!

Why didn't the troll ever invite the billy goats over?
They could be a little gruff.

How do you know when your computer is not well?
It starts hacking.

Why was the controller so upset with the console?
It was playing games with her.

Why did the Playstation take a staycation?
It was sort of tied down.

How did the football like being the star of the game?
It got a kick out of it.

How did one lightning bolt meet the other?
By striking up a conversation.

How do you know when the moon is starstruck?
It's got a little twinkle in its eye.

Why did Mario have to leave work?
He had a fight with the boss.

How do you know your game is leaving you?
It packed, man.

What do goats do on the Web?
They go trolling.

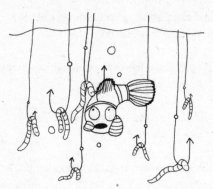

What is Nemo's least favorite game?

Go Fish!

What do gamers order for lunch?
A combo.

What did the video game excel in at track?
The triple jump.

When is it time to feed your video game?
When it starts eyeing the energy bars.

What did the present get for winning the race?
Another ribbon.

What did one gambler say to the other about their odds of winning?
I bet I win.

What is Bruno's favorite planet?
Mars.

Why will John's music be remembered?
Because he's a Legend.

What do you call a fowl kingdom?
A duck dynasty.

Where do Justin and a lumberjack like to go swimming?
In a Timberlake.

What is a star's favorite walk?
On a red carpet.

What's the most talented fish in the ocean?
Starfish.

Why was the actor never down?
He was always acting up.

Why would Tiger Woods make a great sailor?
He's good at staying on course.

What do stars use in their fireplaces?

Holly Wood!

Who named Lady Gaga?
A baby.

What did the feather boa think of the joke?
It was tickled pink.

What movie do elves like to watch?
Gnome Alone.

Why couldn't the famous rapper break a dollar?
Because he was only 50 Cent.

What would Taylor Swift's cat do if she fell in the water?
She would shake it off, off, off.

Why is the villain so good at camping?

Because he's flamous!

Where does Ariana like to go on vacation?
To the Grande Canyon.

Of all the golfers, who do you think will go down in history as the best?
Tiger woulds.

Why was Angelina Jolie?
Because it was the holidays.

Why did the boots have to miss the rodeo?
Someone had kicked their heels up.

Why do cowboys wear cowboy boots?
Because it's tough to ride a horse in ski boots.

What does Jennifer Lopez like for dessert?
JLo.

What did the stirrup say to the boot?
Are you spur you want to ride?

How quickly did the stars notice the paparazzi were gone?
In a flash.

What did the Pony Express put on their envelopes?
Stampedes.

Why didn't the cows go into the river?
Because they moo better.

Why did the cow have to go on a diet?

It was eating like a horse!

How do cowboys rest on the way to the rodeo?

They let the cattle drive!

Why weren't the mountains very hungry?
They had too much desert.

Where do purple dinosaurs live?
In a Barn-ey.

Why wouldn't the cowboy eat his dinner?
They were feeding him grubs.

What did the hunter say that had everyone in the cabin upset?
Bear with me.

Why was the boot so uncomfortable?
He got off on the wrong foot.

Why was the computer so nervous?
It couldn't get with the program.

Why did the doctor keep checking his TV?
To see if it was operational.

Why didn't the nut like the bolt?
Because he was screwed up.

How do clouds communicate?

They Sky-pe!

How did the bed learn to play piano?
Using sheet music.

What do you call it when a computer gets new shoes?
Rebooted.

What did the computer say when the salesperson asked if they could help?
I'm just browsing.

What happened to the light when the switch was feeling down?
It couldn't go on.

Why did the barn fall down?
It wasn't stable.

Why didn't the computer
Know what to do?

It lost its "memory"

Why were there so many lines between the words?
They were spaced out.

How did the dog get its data back?
It retrieved it.

Why do birds make the best scientists?
They already have their own beakers.

Why did the pen write a circle around the word joke?
It was just joking around.

What is a straw's favorite flower?
Two lips.

How do knights change their TV channels?
With a remoat.

Why was the screw so mad?
Because it didn't get its turn.

Where did the computer and the Internet go when they went out?
On a data.

When do movies do what they are told?
On demand.

Why wouldn't the PC talk about its problems?
It was too personal.

Where does the computer's cat like to sleep?

On its lap-top!

What happens if you give the king of the jungle an Xbox?

You get a lion gamer.

How did the computer monitor describe the keyboard?

Kind of touchy.

How will bees get their packages delivered in the future?

By drones.

Why don't phones wear glasses?

They have contacts.

What is something you should never do to your headphones?

Poke them in their iPhone.

What did the computer do after taking a big breath?

It ex-celled.

How did the smartphone get smarter?

It studied its text books.

How can a phone take pictures without anyone else pushing a button?

All by its selfie.

Why did the chicken want a GPS?

To help it get to the other side of the road.

What do you call a phone that won't share?

Cellfish.

What has several keys, numerous windows, and even a mouse but isn't a house?
A computer.

Why did the sewing machine always look busy?
Because that's how it seams.

Why did the couch jump in front of the falling lamp?
To cushion its fall.

What do you call it when one step sues another step?

A stair case.

What do you get when you put your pants on a diet?

Skinny jeans.

What did the windows say to the blinds as they were going away?

I guess it's curtains for us!

What do you call a basement light that won't work?

Down and out.

Why did the stairs have to keep checking the instructions?
Somehow it took the wrong steps.

What are the softest type of crimes to solve?
Pillow cases.

What kind of shoes do sinks hate the most?
Clogs.

How will things turn out for the radio in the future?
Stay tuned.

What was the burglar doing in the bank?
Trying to find a safe place.

Which part of the kitchen is the best at math?

The counter!

How do steps like to compete?
By having stairing contests.

Why did the toilet turn so red?
It was flushed.

What goes undercover but isn't a spy?
Your pajamas.

Why couldn't the TV buy anything?
Because it was flat broke.

What did one flashlight tell the other?
Come ON!

What did the ice do even though someone left the freezer open?
It kept its cool.

What did the dandelions say when the grass asked them to come over?

Weed love to!

What did the drill say at the end of its life?
I sure have been through a lot.

How can you tell when a washing machine is resting?
It takes a load off.

How can you tell when a door isn't going to change its mind?
When it is completely closed to it.

What did the father mower tell his son when life got really hard?
When the mowing gets tough, the tough get mowing!

Why was the picture innocent?
Because it was framed.

What did the fishing pole say when he caught a giant fish?

This just can't be reel!

What kind of nail should you
never hit with a hammer?

Your fingernail!

What did the angry shoes say to the sock?
You stink!

How do you know when your dishes are through?
They are all washed up.

Why did the rug need a haircut?
Because it was shaggy.

How can you tell when a bell was in an accident?
It has a ding in it.

What do houses call chores?
Homework.

What did the demolition crew say about the building?
It's going down.

How did the firefighter become chief?
He climbed the ladder.

Why wasn't the shirt tucked in?
It was just hanging out.

How did the shopping bag get torn?
It was malled.

What did the bathtub give the shower when they got engaged?
A ring.

What happened when the two combs got into a fight?
They parted ways.

How did the water feel about going underground?
It didn't take it well.

What did the baby comb say to the big comb when they bumped into each other?
I'm fine.

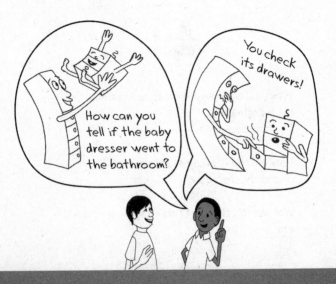

How can you tell if the baby dresser went to the bathroom?

You check its drawers!

What did the thread tell the needle?
Just sew you know, I'm a little tied up.

What did the mother toilet do when the baby toilet wouldn't quit talking?
She put a lid on it.

What did the firefighter think about the fire?
That it was alarming.

What did the concrete blocks do when they met?
Cemented their friendship.

What does a Yes person say all the time?
I don't "no."

Why didn't the motel go out?
It decided to stay inn.

Why was the sun so sad?

It was watching the clouds go bye!

What did they call the rope's sense of humor?
A little twisted.

How did the soda slide under the door?
It was flat.

Who is always very timely?
Your alarm.

What did one alarm clock say to the other alarm clock?
Do you ever hear a ringing in your ears?

How did the chicken react to the joke?
It was a good egg about it.

What did the broom do to the yard stick?

Swept it off its feet!

What would you call it if you sat down on a chewed piece of gum?
A very sticky situation.

Why do doors like nighttime best?
They're knockturnal.

Why did the money seem so different to everyone?
It had changed.

What happened when Santa got the flu?
He made his-elf sick.

How did the shoes find their missing laces?
They ran them down.

Why didn't the bread ever rise?
There was no knead.

What is the favorite game for potatoes and hamburger?
Hash tag.

Why should you always ask for your mother's permission first?
Because your father no's best.

What did the watch say to the scale?
Weight a minute!

What did the pliers do for the drill?
They helped him out a bit.

How did the rope feel when it broke?

It was knot happy!

How can you tell when your scissors get mad?

They're a little snippy!

What comes between before school and after school?
Middle school.

Why couldn't the crayon see anything?
It blacked out!

Why was the ruler so confused?
It couldn't think straight.

What did one ruler say when the other ruler was leaving?
So long!

What do you call it when there's nothing on your math homework?
No problem.

Why couldn't the second class of kids get on the plane?
They only had room for the first class.

Why were the scissors smiling?
Because they had their work cut out for them.

Why did the red marker get in trouble for writing in the book?
Because it red it all by itself.

The Mini Jokiest Joke Book

What are the best steps to take to solve a really hard math problem?
The steps up to your teacher's desk.

Why was the dot-to-dot struggling?
It couldn't seem to connect.

What's another name for counterfeit money?
Play dough.

Why did the newspaper struggle in school?
It was having trouble with its Times tables.

What do you call a thermometer that doesn't pass its test?
A failed a-temp.

Why did the cowboy have to leave school?

For horsing around too much!

Why did the lipstick and mascara
have to stay after school?

To do makeup work!

What do you call dirt that isn't real?
Play ground.

How did the cars do in school?
They didn't pass.

Why did the sheet music do well on a test?
It had taken notes.

How did the eagle do in school?
It soared.

How did the rainbow do in school?
It passed with flying colors.

How did the carpenters do in school?
They finished.

How did the boat do in school?
It sailed through.

How did the road do at coloring?
It stayed inside the lines.

What did the bookshelves do at school?
They learned their upper and lower cases.

How did the shovel do in school?
It ditched a few classes.

Which part of school is a farmer's favorite?
Field trips.

How did the computer programs do in school?
They excelled.

How was school for the traffic light?
A little stop and go.

How was school for the concrete?
Really hard.

Why couldn't Humpty Dumpty wait for winter?
Because he had a great fall.

How did Bob the Builder do in school?
He nailed it.

What's a lawyer's favorite part of school?
Recess.

How did the fireman do in school?
Smoking.

What did the baggie do when the teacher told him no more talking?

He zipped it up!

**Knock, knock. Who's there? I'm kinda.
I'm kinda who?**
I'm kinda tired of knocking, can I come in?

Knock, knock. Who's there? Justin. Justin who?
Justin time to see you.

Knock, knock. Who's there? Can I. Can I who?
Can I just ring your bell the next time?

Knock, knock. Who's there? Ima. Ima who?
Ima gonna go if you don't open the door.

**Knock, knock. Who's there? Don't Chew.
Don't chew who?**
Don't chew want the pizza that you ordered?

Knock, knock. Who's there? Eye. Eye who?
Eye wish the ice cream truck would come by.

Knock, knock. Who's there? Nose. Nose who?
Nose anybody who wants a puppy?

Knock, knock. Who's there? Ear.
Ear who? Ear that?
I think someone is here.

Knock, knock. Who's there? Necks. Necks who?
Necks time I come to the door I'll ring.

Knock, knock. Who's there? Sea. Sea who?
Sea you at the beach.

Knock, knock. Who's there? Hair. Hair who?
Hair I am!

Knock, knock. Who's there? Sneaker.
Sneaker who?
Sneaker in the back door.

Knock, knock. Who's there? Hand. Hand who?
Hand over the pizza.

Knock, knock. Who's there? Boy. Boy who?
Boy it's nice out here.

**Knock, knock. Who's there? Woody.
Woody who?**
Woody like to come out and play ball with me?

**Knock, knock. Who's there? Connie. Connie
who?**
Connie come out and play?

Knock, knock. Who's there? Blue. Blue who?
Blue you, I'm sad.

Knock, knock. Who's there? Sky. Sky who?
Sky was wondering if you want to look at the stars?

Knock, knock. Who's there? Ben. Ben who?
Ben here before.

Knock, knock. Who's there? Wheat. Wheat who?
Wheat a minute, I'll be right in.

Knock, knock. Who's there? Later. Later who?
Later, gator; I'm leaving.

Knock, knock. Who's there? Cheetah. Cheetah who?

Cheetah, you were supposed to be hiding outside.

Knock, knock. Who's there? Rhino. Rhino who?

Rhino who you are.

Knock, knock. Who's there? Owl. Owl who?

Owl have to check.

Knock, knock. Who's there? Schooner. Schooner who?

Schooner or later you have to come out.

Knock, knock. Who's there? Howie. Howie who?

Howie gonna get in if you don't open the door?

Knock, knock. Who's there? Winter. Winter who?

Winter you going to decide?

Knock, knock. Who's there? Surprise.
Surprise who?
Surprise, it's your birthday!

Knock, knock. Who's there? Wreath.
Wreath who?
Wreath me alone, I'm mad.

Knock, knock. Who's there? Justin. Justin who?
Justin time, it's starting to rain.

Knock, knock. Who's there? Linda. Linda who?
Linda me a hand, this box is heavy.

Knock, knock. Who's there? Ima. Ima who?
Ima fraid so please let me in.

Knock, knock. Who's there? Izza. Izza who?
Izza anybody home?

Knock, knock. Who's there? Tag. Tag who?
Tag, you're it!

Knock, knock. Who's there? Ida. Ida who?
Ida called, but I wanted to see you.

Knock, knock. Who's there? Shirley. Shirley who?
Shirley you know who I am.

Knock, knock. Who's there? Whoo. Whoo who?
Whoo hooo, let's have a party!

Knock, knock. Who's there? Olive. Olive who?
Olive us.

Knock, knock. Who's there? Door bell. Door bell who?
Door bell repair person.

Knock, knock. Who's there? Dewey. Dewey who?
Dewey have to keep knocking?

Knock, knock. Who's there? Candace. Candace who?
Candace be real or are we dreaming?

Knock, knock. Who's there? Cara. Cara who?
Cara if I stay for lunch?

Knock, knock. Who's there? Doris. Doris who?
Doris open, do you want me to close it?

Knock, knock. Who's there? Elsa. Elsa who?
Elsa you open this door or I'm leaving.

Knock, knock. Who's there? Eileen. Eileen who?
Eileen on the door, but it still won't open.

Knock, knock. Who's there? Why. Why who?
Why aren't you answering?

Knock, knock. Who's there? Abby. Abby who?
Abby right back, I forgot something.

Knock, knock. Who's there? Ivan. Ivan who?
Ivan standing out here way too long.

Knock, knock. Who's there? Simon. Simon who?
Simon says open the door.

Knock, knock. Who's there? Hope. Hope who?
Hope you don't mind me stopping by.

Knock, knock. Who's there? Isabelle. Isabelle who?
Isabelle broken?

Knock, knock. Who's there? Iva. Iva who?
Iva had enough of you.

Knock, knock. Who's there? Dora. Dora who?
Dora was already open.

**Knock, knock. Who's there? Harriet.
Harriet who?**
Harriet all the birthday cake.

Knock, knock. Who's there? Gwen. Gwen who?
*Gwen are we going to play something other than this
door game?*

Knock, knock. Who's there? Heidi. Heidi who?
Heidi go seek and you're it!

Knock, knock. Who's there? Santa. Santa who?
Santa who can't get down the chimney.

Knock, knock. Who's there? Wyatt. Wyatt who?
Wyatt this house and not yours?

Knock, knock. Who's there? Ima. Ima who?
Ima cold, let me in!

What do you call it when you have brain surgery?

Being open-minded!

What happens when a football team pays too much during a draft?

They get a quarter back.

How do you stop two bats from hitting each other?

Put them in the calm-bat zone.

What did the police officer say to the roller coaster after it came speeding by?

Looks like I'm gonna have to take you for a ride!

How did the bowling ball get into an accident?
By changing lanes.

Why was the clock always late?
It was broken.

How did the detective catch the necklace thief?
Because of the chain of events.

Why did one baseball break up with the other baseball?
They were threw.

Is there anything worse than competing against three professional golfers?
Yes, fore.

How come a baseball has
such a great sense of humor?

It's always in stitches!

What's a golfer's favorite sandwich?
A club.

How did the golfer know he was going to win the game?
A birdie told him.

Why didn't the baseball glove get the flu?
It wasn't catchable.

Where does a down-and-out bowling ball go?
The gutter.

Why didn't the phone answer a lot of the time?
It was disconnected.

What did the phone say at the end of a bad connection?

We're breaking up!

Why did the fisherman hang up on his friend?

Because he had a fish on the other line.

What sport should you be in if you are always mad?

Cross-country.

Why did one phone break up with the other phone?

Because he had too many hang-ups?

Why did everyone think the necklace looked suspicious?

It had bead-y eyes.

What kind of underwear is the toughest?

Boxers!

Why wouldn't the shirt leave the hanger alone?
It was hung up on it.

Why did the football coach cut the clock in half?
It was halftime.

Why was the nose such a bad basketball player?
Because it didn't like to be picked.

How do you catch a volleyball fish?
With a volleyball net.

What's the best way to keep your phone dry?
Wring it out.

Why was the closet pole so mad at the hangers?
They all hung up on him.

How did the basketball team know their player was sick?
He threw up.

Why did the boxer get kicked out of the pool?
For being on the ropes.

Why was the health instructor let go?
Because it was a bad fit.

When did the giants know they had made it?
When they were in the big leagues.

What kind of phones do they use in prison?
Cell phones.

Why couldn't the tree answer the question?

He was stumped!

What did Good Cop have after Lord Business erased his face?
A Blank look.

What do you call it when a tank can't stop?
Un-brake-able.

How did Mator know he needed a change?
He was stuck in a rut.

Where do frogs like to store all their stuff?

On their iPads!

What do you call a truck that wears a size 13 shoe?
Big Foot.

How you keep your pants from falling off their seat?
You belt them in.

Why did the semi have to pull over to sleep?
It was very tire-d.

When can a highway have problems?
When it gets out of line.

Why did the concrete fail the first time?
It didn't try hard enough.

What did the turn signal do
when he couldn't turn right?

He left!

**How did the intersection feel about all of
the traffic?**
Very cross.

Why was the trailer rolling away?
It went off without its hitch.

**What did one ear ask the other when they
reached the intersection?**
Where do we go from hear?

Why did the construction hats have to be apart?
They couldn't work it out.

Where do cars go on vacation?
Cruises.

What did the muffler say after the long trip?

I'm exhaust-ed!

What do you get when you combine a pickup and thunder?
A Big Boom truck.

Why did the turn signal miss the turn?
It blinked.

What do you call racing 24/7?
Life in the fast lane.

What do you call it when your hatchet hits your car?
An axe-i-dent.

How do you know when a tire is well?
It's not slick.

What did the bowling balls do when the lane closed?
They rolled with it.

How did the concrete feel about leaving the blocks?
It was very hard!

Why was the CAUTION sign so smart?
It was SLOW to anger.

What game really messes up traffic?
Red light, green light, red light . . .

What do you call an army officer who crashes his car?
Captain Crunch.

What do racecars do when they get tired?

They crash somewhere for the night!

What did the radio say to the GPS?
I'll follow you anywhere.

Why did the racecar quit altogether?
It was a drag.

How did the car improve its driving?
It took a crash course.

What do you have when you have two people named Lane on the same road?
A two-Lane highway.

Why were the plants so nervous when the flower drove?
It always put the petal to the metal.

Where do all the numbers eat dinner?

At the times table!

Why was the calendar so hard to read?
Its days were all mixed up.

Why was the calendar moving so slowly?
It was feeling week.

What did one hand say to the other when their days were numbered?
I'm counting on you!

Why does the number twelve
always seem so sleepy?

Because it's a doze-n!

**Why couldn't the car door figure out how
to open?**
It couldn't get a handle on it.

Why were the numbers such a problem?
They were always up two something.

**Why weren't the numbers friends with
the magnet?**
They were too negative.

**What did the numbers do with everything at
the times tables?**
They eight it up.

Why was the man's watch on backwards?
It did an about-face.

Why were the math problems
in such good shape?

They did their exercises!

What do baby math problems drink?
Formulas.

Why did the scientist get rid of his clock?
It was a matter of time.

What did the father number call his boy?
My sum.

What did the money say about its change?
It was worth it.

How did the fishermen know there was a mistake on their bill?
They caught it.

How do you get a penny in the mail?
You get one cent.

Why did the money stop by the bank?
It was paying them a visit.

How do pillars talk to their families?
They column.

What do birds retire on?
Their nest eggs.

What do your dishes like to do on Friday nights?
Bowl.

Why was the cow mad at the dart?
For hitting the bull's eye!

What do you call it when two numbers have a baby?
A new addition.

What is something only two equations can have?

A problem child!

Why was the number so proud?
Because everyone counted on him.

Why was math such a problem?
Nothing added up.

Why couldn't the calculator share its lunch?
Because everybody wanted sum.

Why did the mathematician need a ladder?
Things were starting to add up.

What do cowboys do with partial numbers?
They round them up.

What do rabbits like to add?
Hole numbers.

What was the math problem's favorite dessert?

The pie chart!

Why was the compass so frustrated?
It couldn't get the right angle.

What do confused problems ask?
What's the difference?

What do big numbers wear?
Plus-sizes.

How did the students feel about the abacus?
They counted on him.

Why do bunnies do so well in math?
They are very good at multiplying.

Are all numbers the same?
More or less.

How did the gymnasts feel about changing places with the dancers?

They were pretty flexible!

Did the godmother use her wand in time?

Yes, she was fairy fast!

Why did Pinocchio ask so many questions?
He was very nosey.

What do you call a poem you can say over and over again?
A reverse.

What do you get when you combine a rock with a newspaper?
Hard times.

What did Humpty Dumpty do after the fall?
He went to pieces.

What happened after Jack broke his crown?
It all sort of went downhill from there.

Why did Thomas get in trouble at the table?
For chugging down his drink.

What do all of the storybook characters think of Red Riding Hood?
She's cape-able.

What did the Three Little Pigs say when there was no one at the door?
Werewolf?

How long did it take to get rid of the dragon?

Two knights!

The Mini Jokiest Joke Book

Why couldn't Cinderella play baseball?

She was always running away from the ball!

How do clocks start their bedtime stories?
Once upon a time . . .

When did the king ask for the royal joker?
Jest in time.

Which storybook character could be an author?
Little Red Writing Hood.

What did one story say to the other?
You're telling me!

What do you have when you have two ducks and a goose?
A game!

Who did little Miss Peep invite to the dance?

Her Bo!

What did the mirror say to the Queen when Snow White won?
You need to face it.

What did Jack say the second time he went down the hill?
I'm not falling for that again!

How come Jack can never be king?
Because he broke his crown.

Where do you keep a wild squash?
In a zoochini.

How did Alice finally figure out where she was?
She put on her looking glasses.

Why was Baa Baa always getting into trouble?
Because he was the black sheep of the family.

How do you find a book in a hospital?
You page it.

What's the last thing an author will ever write?
The end.

Why wouldn't the artist read the cartoon novel?
It was too graphic.

Why was the story so mad at the writer?
He was plotting against it.

What were Baby Buntings first and last words?
Bye-Bye.

Why can't the three bears ever open the door?

Goldie locks it!

Why was the whole Miss Muffet thing such a drama?

It was an itsy bitsy spider.

Where did Peter Peter's wife go?

The pumpkin eater.

How did the pirate know it was time for tea?

Polly Put the Kettle On.

Why was Wee Willie winking?

He had something in his eye.

Why were the flowers so smart?

The roses are read to.

What do you get when a knight hits his head?

A starry, starry knight!

How do cars eat?

Off their license plates!

Why did Mr. Potato Head look so sad?
Because his mouth was on upside down.

Why did the circus performer get so tired at work?
He was juggling two jobs.

What kind of haircuts do sponges get?
Bobs.

Why did the snake get lost?

It was rattled!

What do you get when you combine a pirate and a bird?
A Jack Sparrow.

What do you get when you cross Bozo with a goldfish?
A clown fish.

How does Count Dracula play baseball?
With a vampire bat.

Why was Mr. Potato Head so embarrassed?
He picked someone else's nose.

What is Shaggy's favorite hobby?
Scooby diving.

What do you call Princess Sofia's problems?

A royal mess!

If a mountain and a valley had a baby, what would they name it?
Cliff.

What is Anna and Elsa's favorite game?
Freeze tag.

What happens when Sponge Bob pretends to be a pirate?
He walks the plankton.

Which bunny can drive you crazy?
Bugs.

What did Puss do when someone complimented his shoes?
He gave them the boot.

Why was the tree so loud?

It had a lot of bark!

How did Donatello the Ninja Turtle finally get a girlfriend?
He finally came out of his shell.

How did the Seven Dwarfs feel about being short?
They under-stood completely.

What was the first thing Thomas did with his dog when he brought it home?
He trained it.

Why did the king believe the knight's story?
He sword it was true.

What did the skunk say to the only pink cat it had ever seen?
Hello, kitty.

How can you tell if a cartoon is happy?
It's very animated.

Where do chicken jokes come from?
The funny farm.

What one word can change everything?
Abracadabra.

What do you call a clown who wears his nose on his ear?
A Bozo.

Why are pickles so slow?
They tend to dill-y-dally.

Did the turkeys believe the story?

They gobbled it up!

Where do pigs go to get clean?
The hogwash.

Where did Loopsy go on her trip?
To La La Land.

How do canyons eat?
They gorge themselves.

Why was the door so nervous?
It was unhinged.

How did the pig get out of the mud?
It was snort of a problem.

When is your hair noisy?
When it has bangs.

Why was the bowling ball wet?

There was rain in the gutters

Why was Yes always in trouble?
It didn't "no."

How does your laundry solve its problems?
It just sorts them out.

Why was the punctuation put in time-out?
It wouldn't comma down.

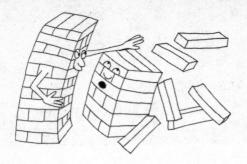

Why was one game of Jenga mad at the other?

It knocked its blocks off!

Why did the drill have to go in a different drawer of the toolbox?
It bit someone.

What did the captain do when his ship ran into trouble?
He re-PORT-ed it.

What did the earthquake say when it was blamed for all the mess?
It wasn't my fault.

What do you do when a clock is bad?
You give it a time-out.

What did one screw tell the other when they ran into a problem?
Use your head.

Why was the witch moving a stick around in her cauldron?

She was trying to stir up trouble.

Why was the little brain sent to its room?

To think about what it did.

Why did Merry go round?

The other rides were in the way.

What kind of cleanser do dogs hate the most?

Spot remover.

Why was Santa having such a problem at the workshop?

He couldn't control his elf.

Why was everyone laughing at the pet shop?

Someone asked "what did that dog doo?"

What do you call a dog that isn't potty trained?

Puddles!

What did the piggy bank say when it was mad?
Save it!

How did Nemo learn his lesson?
He had a little schooling.

What caused the commotion in the washing machine?
One of the pieces of clothing socked the other!

How did the submarine answer the question?
I sink so.

Why did the toilet get into trouble?
It ran in the bathroom.

How do you know when a notebook is in trouble?
It's in a bind.

Did you read the book about the hammer?
It was a nail-biter.

Why did the piece of paper get mad at the pen?
It was out of line.

What do you call it if you are in trouble more than once?
Two much trouble.

Who takes care of the problems in the bathroom?
The toilet handles them.

Why was the pan struggling with her problem?
She didn't know how to handle it.

How do you get a shoe to stop talking?

You put a sock in it!

Why did the pen get into so much trouble?
It was dotting the T's and making the I's cross.

Did you hear about the gum and the dryer?
It was kind of a sticky situation.

Why couldn't the lolli ever be a balloon?
Because the lolli popped.

How did the glasses know the clock was late?
They were watching him.

What did the balloon say right before the party?
I hope this isn't a blowout.

What did the dartboard say to the bad dart player?

What's the point?!

How did the carrot know the onion was hurt?

He was crying!

Why can you never tell lettuce that she's pretty?
Because it always goes to her head.

What does a really bad cold put on its pancakes?
Cough syrup.

Why did the blender chop up the cubes?
It just wanted to break the ice.

What do your arms and cherries have in common?
They both have pits.

What time do cookies hate the most of all?
Crunch time.

Where does really, really dry cake live?
The dessert.

Why was the hen too tired to lay more eggs?
Because she was cooped.

Why was the dough off by itself?
It kneaded to be alone.

Why did the butter always lose?
Because it was creamed.

Why did the lettuce take the bus?
Because it had to leaf.

What did the one straw say to the other straw when times got tough?
Suck it up.

Why didn't the bread rise?
There was no knead.

What do you get when you mix sheet music with syrup?
Sticky notes.

How did the banana get away fast?

It peeled out of the kitchen!

What made the pickles' lives so bumpy?

They were a little jarred!

How quickly did the pudding and milk become friends?
Almost instantly.

What kind of water never runs downstream?
Bottled water.

Where do ice like to get together to work?
In a cube-ical.

What's the funniest thing about an egg?
Its yolk.

Why were the melons laughing?
They were having a ball.

How do you see a cabbage in the dark?
Head lights.

How do you get information from a hamburger?
You grill it.

Why are people so sleepy after they eat?
They're at a rest-aurant.

What kind of water doesn't pour?
Ice.

Why was the fruit salad mad at the grapes?
They were raisin trouble.

Why was the potato creepy?
It kept an eye on everyone.

Who do the chocolate bunnies hang out with at Easter?
Their peeps.

What did one pretzel say to the other?

Why are you so twisted?

Why did the cake go shopping all the time?

Its frosting was really rich!

What did the bread say when it was put in the oven?
I'm toast!

Why was the plum so upset?
It got pruned.

What did the spaghetti say to the macaroni?
You look a little bent out of shape.

What happened to the cabbage?
It laughed its head off.

What did the corn call their leader?
Kernel.

How did the peach know it needed glasses?
Things were getting a little fuzzy.

15
ZOOLARIOUS—
Jokes About Animals, etc.

What do you get when you combine a monkey, a scholar, and some bananas?
A bunch of bananas that know better than to monkey around.

What do you get when you cross a dog with a bull?
A best friend who can always give you a buck.

What did the baby duck do when its parents went to see the doctor?
It stayed in the wading room.

Where do horses live?
In their neigh-borhood.

How do frogs die?
They croak.

What did the horse say when the cow tried to take its food?
Hay!

What do you get when you cross a pig's tail with a potato?
Curly fries.

What do you get when you cross a cow and a toad?

A bullfrog!

What happens when you mix a pig with a fishing rod?
It becomes a reel ham.

What do you get when you put a Chihuahua in a pile of leaves?
Dog gone if I know.

What do you get when you give a chimpanzee a TV?
A swing set.

What do elephants always take to the pool?
Their trunks.

What do you get when you cross a coyote and a primate?

A howler monkey!

What kind of fish is the best hugger?

A cuttlefish!

What do you get when you mix a lamb with a yellow jacket?
A really sharp wool coat.

What do you call a cross between a kangaroo and a legume?
A jumping bean.

What do you get when you cross a fly with Bigfoot?
A fly that can swat you.

What do cows use when they drive?
Bull horns.

What kind of underwear do dogs wear?
Boxers.

What kind of shark is the handiest?

How do you hide a camel?
You use camelflage.

What do Santa's deer wear when it's really wet outside?
Reincoats.

Why was the kangaroo in a bad mood?
It was feeling a little pouchy.

What did the fish have to wear to class everyday?
A school uniform.

What kind of sweaters do tortoises wear?
Turtlenecks.

What do you get when you cross a Chihuahua and a skunk?
A dog that's a little stinky.

What do you get when you mix a poodle and a porcupine?
A dog that's a little prickly about its haircut.

What do you get when you mix an eel with a quilt?
An electric blanket.

What do you get when you cross a cobra and a plant?
Poison ivy.

Why couldn't the zebra sing?
Because it was hoarse.

How did one porcupine make the other porcupine laugh?

It was acting quilly!

Why couldn't the joke get around very well?

It was lame.

What can appear, disappear, and reappear whenever it wants?

The word "appear."

When the land and the water were arguing, which side did the shell take?

The sea's side.

Why did one woodpecker think the other was sick?

He looked a little peckish.

Why did the volcano never erupt?

Because it was a lava not a hater.

Why was the lightning so bad at bowling?

Lightning never strikes twice.

Why did the chicken have to go to time-out?

Because of its fowl language.

What kind of card does a frog
use when it goes shopping?

Debbit!

How did the puzzle get itself together?
It just sort of fell into place.

Why were the shoes going backwards?
They were retracing their steps.

Why didn't the drum ever lose?
It couldn't be beat.

How come the camera couldn't concentrate?
It lost focus.

What decision did the tree have to make?
Take it or leaf it.

What do you call a really mean cow?
A Bully.

What part of a candy bar likes music the most?

The wrapper!

Where do most lions live?
On Mane Street.

Why was the balloon getting so tired?
It had been up all night.

How did the swimmer win the lottery?
She had a stroke of luck.

How do the nuts get anything accomplished?
They get cracking.

Why did the cough drop quit?
It couldn't hack it anymore.

Why couldn't the margarine do its job?
It wouldn't stick to it.

Why did the fingernail lose the race?
It wasn't that quick.

Why did the doctor have to check the treasure?
It was having chest pains.

What do you call a fake deer?
A play doe.

How did they know the chimney was sick?
It had a flue.

Why did one flower get mad at the other flower?
It wouldn't leaf.

Why did the Post-it have to leave its job?

It couldn't stick to its work!

What do you get when you
put a clock in the trash?

A waste of time!

When can you get lost in the corn?
When it's a maize.

Which academy did the orange attend?
The navel academy.

How do dogs take a break from their movies?
They paws them.

What did the jet think of its trip?
It was sort of plane.

How do you get a flower to stay put?
You planter.

Who is the hungriest superhero of all?

Supperman!

What do superheroes do when things don't go their way?
POW-t.

Why doesn't Batman play cards?
He doesn't want anything to do with the Joker.

How did the parachutes get tricked?
They fell for it.

How do you get snow out of the air?

Use a skyscraper!

What do you get when you put one night above another?
An over nighter.

Why did the superhero save the chicken?
Because it tried to cross the road at rush hour.

What kind of beam can you never walk across?
A beam of light.

What do superheroes use to fix their ripped disguises?
Masking tape.

What did the sun say to the cloud?
I'm going to shine weather you like it or not.

Which superhero is the most curious?

Wonder Woman!

What did the rocket say to Earth?
I'm gonna have to take off now.

What did one mallard say to the other when a low-flying plane came by?
Duck!

Why did the rocket fall over?
It was a little off base.

What kind of bolt never needs a nut?
A lightning bolt.

Where did the mist go?
It vanished into thin air.

What did the cheese call the sandwich?
My hero.

Why was the sleet in bed?
It was under the weather.

How did Buzz do in space?
He went above and beyond.

How did the ocean keep its floor?
Very tidy.

How do galaxies work out?
On their ellipticals.

Which one of Santa's reindeer flies the highest?
Comet.

What would happen if a thief stole everyone's clocks?

They would have all the time in the world!

Why was the wind always poor?

It blew all of its money!

How does a barber trim a planet's hair?
Eclipse it.

Why did the galaxy fall apart?
It spiraled out of control.

Why did the door leave the ball game?
Someone knocked it out of the park.

Why was the sun getting richer?
Because of its raise.

What did the sun say to the moon?
You're looking a little shady.

Why don't olives like being eaten?
It's the pits.

What do you call an old rocket?
A blast from the past.

What happens if you embarrass a planet?
It turns red.

What happens when the moon hits its head?
It sees stars.

Where does the earth keep all of its trophies?
On its mantle.

What does the moon put its cheese on?
A crescent roll.

Why did the spaceship miss the moon?

He didn't planet very well!

18
DEEP THOUGHTS—
Jokes for Brainiacs, etc.

Why couldn't the bulb light up?

It had no ideas!

Why did everyone think the present was the smartest thing going?
It was gifted.

What do the words "behind," "tail," and "rear" have in common?
They are all back words.

Why did the fishing pole know all the answers?
It was a reel thinker.

What did the brain ask the machine?
M R I all right?

What do the North Pole and the South Pole have in common?
Nothing, they're polar opposites.

Why couldn't the skull think?
It was a no-brainer.

Why did the cauliflower struggle with putting the puzzle together?
It couldn't wrap its head around it.

Why did the cards have to quit the game?
Someone realized they weren't playing with a full deck.

The Mini Jokiest Joke Book

Why wouldn't the duck fly away?

It was rubber!

Which kind of water has the most emotion?
The ocean, because it is so deep.

What kind of break doesn't hurt?
Spring break.

What has to go down before you can get up?
Your fever.

What do you get when you take the "hi" out of history?
Just another story.

How can you make the word "gone" go away?
Put the word "all" in front of it.

Why was the egg so confused?

It was scrambled!

How did the rope come untied?
They're knot sure.

How did the rhino let the other animals know they were in its way?
It used its horn.

What was the baby wearing on its face when it was born?
Nothing but a smile.

How many ways can you say the same thing?
One: "the same thing."

What did one brain ask the other?
What do you think?

What does one brain do when it sees another?
It waves.

In what ways can something last forever?
All-ways.

How do bridges handle things that get too deep?
They get over it.

Why did the ocean have to calm down?
It was making waves.

How did the magician make all of his problems go away?
With a little hocus pocus.

What do you call a tired snail?
Sluggish.

What season is the clumsiest?

Fall!

What do beds do when their work is all done?
They retire.

Why was the hair so upset?
Someone told a blonde joke.

Where can you find sad trash?
Down in the dumps.

What kitchen object is the sharpest?
The cleaver.

What do skunks use to help themselves survive?
Their in-stinks.

What can be both hot and cold?
Chilly chili.

What kind of story would a ghostwriter write?
A spooky one.

What do you call it when a baby vampire crawls?
A little creepy.

Why do zombies walk so slow?
Because they're dead tired.

What do mad mops do?

Kick the bucket!

How do you know if you're a ghost?
When food goes right through you.

What do baby zombies wear?
Die-pers.

What do you call zombie phones?
Dead ringers.

How do you know when two zombies are talking?
It's dead quiet.

What do little spirits like before bed?
Ghost stories.

What does a ghost say when you knock at the door?
Boo is it?

How do you know when a poltergeist is scared?
He's white as a ghost.

How did the skeleton get in the house?
It used its key.

What do you say to a zombie without a brain?
Nevermind.

How can you be sure when a zombie isn't right?
When they're dead wrong.

Why did one dog get mad at the other dog?

They had a bone to pick!

What does a ghost call its favorite person?

My Boo!

Why couldn't the stone be a grave marker?
It couldn't get a head.

What did the skeleton think of the grave?
It was a little shallow at times.

What would happen if someone took everything out of the freezer?
Ice cream.

How did the glass know everything was going to be all right?
There was a light at the end of the funnel.

Why does it take longer for a two-headed monster to answer a question?
It has to think twice.

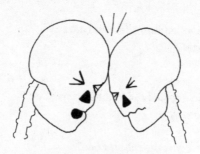

What do skeletons get
when they bump their heads?

Numbskulls!

How did the milk know its time had come?
It was ready to expire.

Why couldn't the skeleton laugh?
He was missing his funny bone.

What do you call someone with a hat made out of bones?
Bonehead.

Why did the zombie stop its car?
It reached a dead end.

Do zombies ever rest?
Of corpse they don't.

What do a bunch of ghosts playing baseball have?
Team spirit.

What is a skeleton's favorite part of Thanksgiving?
The wishbone.

What do ghosts read in their spare time?
Booooooooks.

How long was the rabbit gone?
The hole day.

Why were the skeletons shocked when they looked in the grave?
No body was there.

How did all the colors become extinct?
They all dyed out.

Why are skeletons so hard?

They were scared stiff!

What do you call it when electricity marries gas?

A power couple!

What did the hair do when it all fell out?
It bald.

What did the plank say after lying around all day?
I'm board.

What four letters can get you out of trouble?
HELP.

What did the diamond think of the ruby?

She was a real gem!

What did the letters say when the phone rang?
L, O.

How did the alphabet do on its tests?
It got an A, B, and a C.

What happens if U doesn't win?
U loses.

Which three letters make you hungry just thinking about them?
P, B, and J.

What did the paper say to the tape?
Let's wrap this up!

How did the horse take losing its shoes?
It felt defeeted.

What did the ocean say to the bay as it left?
Sea you soon.

What kind of dance do dots do?
The polka.

Why did the bird take a nap?
It needed a little down time.

What do cold geese get?
Goosebumps.

Why aren't robbers funny?
They can't take a joke.

What did the clock do for the dancer?
She gave him a big hand.

Why did the pan stop hanging around the plastic wrap?

It was too clingy!

What did the backpack tell the
jogging shoes when they broke up?

Take a hike!

What did one buffalo say to the other buffaloes?
I herd you were coming to town!

Why did the eyes do so well in their business?
They were never closed.

How do you kiss a moth?
With butterfly kisses.

How do you know when a tub is married?
It has a ring.

What did the two ropes do at their wedding?
They tied the knot.

**Who did the salad want to marry: the croutons
or the dressing?**
It was a toss-up.

What kind of boat never needs water?

A dreamboat!

How did it go for the pie and the cake?
They loved each other to pieces.

Why was the trash so hurt by the can?
She dumped him.

What did the two pieces of bread give each other on their first date?
A toast.

What does an aunt do if she can't get married?
Antelope.

Who are the most romantic of the fruits?
The dates.

Why didn't the socks stay together?

They weren't a good match!

What did the finger think of the thumb?
It was handsome.

How did the polish feel about the mop?
It took a shine to it.

How could you tell the pickles were fond of one another?
The relished each other.

What did music say when the lyric asked if it would go out?
Of chords I will.

Who broke the dish's heart?
Someone named Chip.